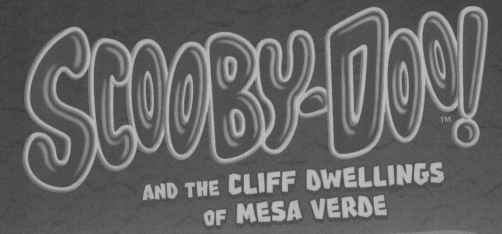

SCOOBY-DOO!

AND THE CLIFF DWELLINGS OF MESA VERDE

THE GHOSTLY GAZE

BY MARK WEAKLAND

Consultant: Julie Markin, PhD
Assistant Professor of Anthropology
Washington College

CAPSTONE PRESS
a capstone imprint

T0051060

In the office of Mystery Incorporated, Daphne was talking on her cell phone.

"We'll be there right away," she said, ending the call. "That was Ranger Chavez from Mesa Verde National Park. She needs our help. Tourists are seeing ghost eyes in the park's cliff dwellings."

"It sounds like we've got a mystery!" said Fred.

Velma brought up a map on her tablet.

Mesa Verde is in the Four Corners region of the United States. The area is full of canyons, cliffs, and mesas.

That's a lot to investigate. We'd better get going.

SCOOBY FACT

The Four Corners region is where the states of Utah, Arizona, Colorado, and New Mexico meet. The region covers about 10,000 square miles (25,900 square kilometers).

UTAH
COLORADO
ARIZONA
NEW MEXICO

The next day the gang piled into the Mystery Machine and drove to meet Ranger Chavez. When they arrived at the park, the gang looked around. The place was empty.

"Welcome to Mesa Verde National Park," said Ranger Chavez, walking up to the group.

"Like, where is everybody?" asked Shaggy.

"People are too afraid to come to the park," said the ranger sadly. "The ghost eyes are keeping visitors away."

"We're here to help, Ranger Chavez," said Daphne.

"Then follow me to the cliff dwellings," said Ranger Chavez as she walked into the park.

"Come on, gang," said Fred. "Maybe we'll see a pair of these eyes for ourselves."

"Like, I hope not!" said Shaggy nervously.

The gang's first stop in their investigation was the Balcony House.

"The Balcony House was built into the side of this cliff beneath a rocky overhang," explained the ranger. "The only way inside is to climb up this 32-foot ladder."

"Radder?" said Scooby, looking scared.

"Come on, Scooby," said Daphne. "You can do it!"

SCOOBY FACT

The Balcony House was built 600 feet (183 meters) above the bottom of Soda Canyon.

The gang climbed to the top and stood
inside the Balcony House's courtyard.

The ancestral Puebloan people built these cliff dwellings. They are the ancestors of today's Pueblo Indians in Arizona and New Mexico.

They lived on top of this mesa for centuries.

That's right, Velma. They began building pueblos like this in the late 1100s.

"The park contains nearly 600 cliff dwellings," said Ranger Chavez. "Most of them are small, with one to five rooms inside. The Balcony House is bigger. It has 38 rooms."

"Like, why would the ancestral Puebloans live on the side of a cliff?" asked Shaggy, scratching his head.

"The springs here provided water during times of drought," said Ranger Chavez. "The cliffs gave shelter from the hot summer sun and the cold winter. They also protected the people from hostile intruders."

RINTRUDERS?

I sure hope we don't see any ghost intruders.

As the gang walked toward the next dwelling, Fred looked at the landscape.

This place doesn't look like a desert.

It's dry here, but there's enough water for plants and trees to grow.

From a lookout point, the gang saw the Spruce Tree House in the distance.

"When the ancestral Puebloans lived in these cliff dwellings, they still farmed on the mesa tops," said Ranger Chavez. "They grew corn and beans and raised turkeys. They also ate wild plants."

Shaggy's stomach began to growl. As the others walked ahead, Shaggy whispered to Scooby. "Like, all this talk of food is making me hungry. Let's go find a bite to eat."

"Reah!" said Scooby, licking his lips. They snuck away to find a snack while the rest of the gang continued to the Spruce Tree House.

Daphne, Velma, and Fred continued to follow Ranger Chavez to the Spruce Tree House. Once inside the ruins, the ranger opened her guidebook. She showed the gang a painting of what life was like there long ago.

SCOOBY FACT

The people who lived in the cliff dwellings wove baskets, made pottery, and prepared food. Larger homes had room to store food and items that could be traded.

"Between 60 and 80 people lived in Spruce Tree House," said Ranger Chavez. "Each family had a small, simple place to live. There was a hearth with a fire hole so the smoke could escape. The ancestral Puebloans often entered their homes through the roofs, using wooden ladders instead of stairs."

"How did the ancestral Puebloans build these places, Ranger Chavez?" asked Fred.

"They used sandstone, mortar, and wooden beams," said Ranger Chavez. "Then the walls were covered with plaster that was tinted brown, red, pink, or white."

Velma scanned the Spruce Tree House. "We've searched the Balcony House and Spruce Tree House, but still no ghost eyes. Have you seen anything, Shaggy and Scooby?" Velma asked, turning behind her. "Jinkies! Where are Shaggy and Scooby?"

"Oh no," said Daphne. "They're probably out looking for food. We'd better find them before something else does."

"I'll look for them," said Ranger Chavez. "You three continue to Cliff Palace. Here, take my guidebook. I'll meet you there."

SCOOBY FACT

Inside the mortar, the ancient people added tiny pieces of stone called chinking. The chinking stones filled in the gaps in the mortar and added more stability to the walls.

Meanwhile Shaggy and Scooby were lost.

Hiking along a trail, they came upon an enormous dwelling. Scooby's eyes grew wide.

This must be Cliff Palace. I've heard about this place. It is the largest dwelling in the park. Let's go see if there is a snack stand in there somewhere.

"Nothing," said Shaggy, disappointed. "Like, there's not even a vending machine out here. Maybe someone left a candy bar around these kivas."

"Rivas?" asked Scooby.

"Those round holes are what's left of the kivas," said Shaggy. "The biggest ones were called great kivas. They were used for public meetings. People gathered inside and talked about important issues. Kivas were also used for religious ceremonies."

SCOOBY FACT

Cliff Palace has 150 rooms and 23 kivas.

"Raggy, rut's rat?" asked Scooby, looking at a pair
of large eyes glaring down from a window.

Velma, Fred, and Daphne walked toward Cliff Palace. Velma held the guidebook that Ranger Chavez had given them.

These cliff dwellings are incredible. I wonder why the ancestral Puebloans left.

"No one knows for sure why these dwellings were abandoned," said Velma, reading the guidebook. "It says here it could have been for a number of reasons. For many years the region suffered droughts. The people may have fought each other over food and water. Archeologists also discovered arrowheads in the area. This could mean that outside tribes attacked the ancestral Puebloans."

"By 1300 the ancestral Puebloan people had left the cliff dwellings," Daphne added. "In another hundred years, these homes had fallen into disrepair and the cliff dwellings were forgotten."

It was getting late as Fred, Daphne, and Velma arrived at Cliff Palace.

If the ancestral Puebloan people moved away, how were the cliff dwellings discovered?

"In 1888 two local ranchers named Richard Wetherill and Charles Mason were searching for their stray cattle," said Velma. "They saw a city made of stone in the distance. They climbed to the ruins and found Cliff Palace."

Velma continued. "Wetherill took thousands of artifacts from Cliff Palace and other areas. Over the years, other visitors took artifacts too. Mesa Verde National Park was created to protect this archeological site.'"

Shaggy and Scooby ran away from the ghost eyes — and straight into Velma. They crashed into each other with a thud.

"Ow!" said Velma.

"Rorry, Relma," said Scooby.

"There you guys are," said Fred, walking up to Scooby, Shaggy, and Velma on the ground. "Where have you been?"

"Like, running away from that!" gasped Shaggy, pointing to a pair of eyes above them.

The gang looked up as two owls came out of the
shadows. Just then Ranger Chavez arrived.

"Is that what was scaring everyone?" the ranger asked.
"Those aren't ghosts. They're Mexican spotted owls."

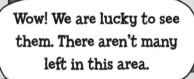

Wow! We are lucky to see
them. There aren't many
left in this area.

"Preserving this area is important work," said Ranger Chavez, looking at the owls. Then she turned and gave Scooby a pat on the head. "And so is solving this mystery. Thank you, Scooby-Doo!"

SCOOBY SNACK-SIZED FACTS

○ Cliff Palace is thought to be the largest cliff dwelling in all of North America.

○ Tower House is a structure within Cliff Palace. It is 26 feet (8 m) tall. It is the tallest building in Mesa Verde.

○ In addition to the rare Mexican spotted owl, other animals live within Mesa Verde. These animals include Abert's squirrels, Colorado pikeminnows, and peregrine falcons.

○ President Theodore Roosevelt created Mesa Verde National Park in 1906.

○ The park and the dwellings have survived numerous wildfires. The most recent wildfire was in 2003.

GLOSSARY

ancestor (AN-sess-tur)—a member of your family who lived a long time ago

artifact (ART-uh-fakt)—an object made or changed by human beings, especially a tool or weapon used in the past

drought (DROUT)—a long spell of very dry weather

dwelling (DWEL-ing)—the place where a person lives

hearth (HARTH)—the area in front of a fireplace

kiva (KEE-vah)—an ancestral Puebloan ceremonial structure that is usually round and partly underground

mesa (MAY-suh)—a hill or mountain with steep sides and a flat top

plaster (PLASS-tur)—a substance used by builders to put a smooth finish on walls or ceilings; today's plaster is made of lime, sand, and water

preserve (pri-ZURV)—to protect something so that it stays in its original state

pueblo (PWEB-loh)—a village consisting of stone and adobe buildings built next to and on top of each other; pueblos were built by American Indian tribes in the southwestern United States

sandstone (SAND-stohn)—a kind of rock made up mostly of sandlike grains of quartz cemented together by lime or other materials

READ MORE

Blake, Kevin. *Cliff Dwellings: A Hidden World.* Abandoned! Towns without People. New York: Bearport Publishing, 2015.

Fay, Gail. *Secrets of Mesa Verde: Cliff Dwellings of the Pueblo.* Archeological Mysteries. North Mankato, Minn.: Capstone Press, 2015.

Meinking, Mary. *What's Great About Colorado?* Our Great States. Minneapolis: Lerner Publications Company, 2015.

INTERNET SITES

Use FactHound to find Internet sites related to this book.

Visit *www.facthound.com*

Just type in 9781515775119 and go.

 Super-cool stuff! Check out projects, games and lots more at
www.capstonekids.com

INDEX

Published in 2018 by Capstone Press, a Capstone Imprint
1710 Roe Crest Drive
North Mankato, Minnesota 56003
www.mycapstone.com

Library of Congress Cataloging-in-Publication Data
Names: Weakland, Mark, author.
Title: Scooby-Doo! and the cliff dwellings of Mesa Verde : the ghostly gaze / by Mark Weakland.
Description: North Mankato, Minnesota : Capstone Press, 2018. | Series: Scooby-Doo!. Unearthing ancient civilizations with Scooby-Doo!

Identifiers: LCCN 2017034027 (print) | LCCN 2017038078 (ebook) | ISBN 9781515775195 (eBook PDF) | ISBN 9781515775119 (library binding) | ISBN 9781515775157 (paperback.)
Subjects: LCSH: Indians of North America—Southwest, New. | Cliff-dwellings—Southwest, New. | Pueblo Indians. | Mesa Verde National Park (Colo.)
Classification: LCC E78.S7 (ebook) | LCC E78.S7 W38 2018 (print) | DDC 979.004/97—dc23
LC record available at https://lccn.loc.gov/2017034027

Editorial Credits:
Editor: Michelle Hasselius
Designer: Ted Williams
Art Director: Nathan Gassman
Production Specialist: Laura Manthe

Design Elements:
Shutterstock: natashasha

The illustrations in this book were created traditionally, with digital coloring.

TITLES IN THIS SET